Poetry for PSHE

Poetry

for

PSHE

A Selection of Poems with Lesson Plans for Secondary Schools

JAY CLARKE

Matador
9 Priory Business Park
Kibworth Beauchamp
Leicestershire LE8 0RX, UK
Tel: (+44) 116 279 2299
Email: books@troubador.co.uk
Web: www.troubador.co.uk/matador

ISBN 978 1784624 576

British Library Cataloguing in Publication Data.
A catalogue record for this book is available from the British Library.

Typeset in 11pt Aldine401 BT by Troubador Publishing Ltd, Leicester, UK
Printed and bound by CPI Group (UK) Ltd, Croydon, CR0 4YY

Matador is an imprint of Troubador Publishing Ltd

For Jonathan – husband, help and in-house audience.

*Also for Jacqui, for whom the poem "School Days" was written, while she
bravely fought her unforgiving illness.
"Carefree days, ours to waste,
Over now, with too much haste".*

Contents

Resources

Preface

"You don't have to suffer to be a poet; adolescence is enough suffering for anyone".

John Ciardi

The first poem in this book is called "The Bully and the Bullied" and it was written a few years ago, as a result of me being given 24 hours to prepare a lesson for a class of 11-12 year old boys on the subject of bullying.

I was a (new) supply teacher and I was told that the boys were having a "PSHE" lesson, a subject I'd never heard of at the time (having long since left school myself), but discovered it stood for Personal, Social, Health and Economic education. As a hobby poet, I thought the easiest – not to mention quickest – way to prepare was to fire off a poem about a bully. I had an idea that I'd call two boys out to the front of the class and ask them to read it. That then gave me the idea of separating the poem into a "dual poem", where they each had their own lines to read, coming from opposing sides. I knew that I had to write for both the bully and the person being bullied. I had no problem getting two volunteers, when I announced, at the beginning of the lesson, that I needed two boys to come up to the front of the class to "have a fight". The boys were engaged immediately and the class was a great success. Coincidentally, I was being assessed at the time for my formal teaching qualifications and here's what my tutor wrote: *"The lesson was delivered as per the session plan. To begin with, a member from each group read out a poem, one reading the part of the bully, the other the bullied. The whole group reviewed the good and bad points from the poem. The next part surprised me, as I would never have believed I'd see a group of 11-12 year old boys so enthused about writing a poem let alone practically begging to read it out".* I knew I had found a way to engage a difficult class.

My guess is, had I asked those boys prior to the lesson whether they liked poetry, there would have been a resounding "no". Being a lover of poetry, however, I know from that experience and many others since, that when young people can really engage with a poem, they learn to love the genre, which is useful, as my long-held ambition is to get teenagers to love poetry. It is no coincidence, therefore, that most of the poems in this book are short and written in rhyming couplet form. In my years of experience, this has been the most effective way of achieving such an engagement. I have worked with children with special educational needs, as well as those who have been excluded from mainstream schools. I can vouch for the effectiveness of planning lessons around simple, short poems such as these, making them enjoyable for even the most ardent initial objector.

The second poem "School Days" wasn't actually written for school children, but for an old school-friend I had lost touch with 30 years ago, who made contact via a social network, only to tell me that they had a terminal illness. I felt so shocked and saddened, that I did the first thing I normally do at such times and wrote a poem that I hoped would resonate and, even only temporarily, cheer them up. I thought it warranted being included because of the subject matter and because I believe it will encourage students to try to imagine how they will think about school retrospectively, once they are grown up. I don't expect them to imagine for a moment how quickly life will pass them by. We only know that once we are grown up ourselves!

Apart from bullying, the subject matter covers schools, families, relationships and confidences. Lesson plans are included for each poem, as appendices at the back of the book, although these are not obligatory and you may build your own plan, as you see fit. There will be a poem in this book for most subjects covered in PSHE and I can guarantee that you will give an enjoyable lesson, which will stay with your students and make them look forward to their next lesson.

1

The Bully and the Bullied

(For two readers)

The Bully   *The Bullied*

1 People like you make me want to throw up,
2 I'll beat you up when we're on the school bus.

3 *What have I done?*
4 *Where does your violence come from?*

5 I don't know why I hate you,
6 I just do.

7 *This isn't fair,*
8 *I've done nothing to you.*

9 Do I look as if I care?
10 It's your name, your style, the clothes you wear.

11 *Why do you care,*
12 *What clothes I wear?*

13 You just don't get it,
14 You're such a nerd.

15 *I help you in class,*
16 *And with your homework*

17 Shut your mouth and watch what you say,
18 Or I won't even wait 'til the end of the day!

The Bully	The Bullied

| | 19   *You're so ungrateful,* |
| | 20   *Why are you acting this way?* |

21   You think you're so clever,
22   Well, I'll show you you're not.

                                            23   *I was willing to help you,*
                                            24   *You've had all that I've got*

25   See, you just don't get it
26   You can't see what I'm after.

                                            27   *I'm the same as you,*
                                          28   *But I just learn faster.*

29   People like you…
30   You get all that you want

                                            31   *I'd give you it all, if I could,*
                                            32   *But I can't*

33   So there's nothing for me,
34   But to make your life hell

                                            35   *So there's nothing for me,*
                                            36   *But to wait for the bell…*

2

Safe House

Nearly there, not long to go,
Are they close behind me? I really think so.

The enemy is almost at the door, but so am I,
Can I keep up the pace? I'm going to try.

Once I get there, I know I'll be safe,
But tomorrow? Tomorrow's another race.

I'll be back on their ground; they rule there.
I don't stand a chance, it doesn't seem fair.

There's no-one to help me, they've made that clear,
If I go to the teachers, I'll end up in tears.

But never mind tomorrow, it's now I need strength,
To get to my safe house; one more street's length.

I won't turn around; I can feel that they're near,
If I shouted for help, would anyone hear?

I long for the weekend, without this race,
To go out, and walk home, at my own slow pace

I'm almost there, where I know I'll be safe,
Almost home, in my own safe place.

3

School Days

I thought about school the other day,
I used to call for my friend on the way.
There was never enough time, we were usually late,
For us, the school bell wouldn't wait!

We'd talk of unfinished essays, DJs, the latest craze,
Anything we thought would fill our boring days.
Wouldn't it be great when there was no more school?
No need to obey other people's rules.

Of course, we knew it all, or so we thought,
But what we should have known could never be taught.
Carefree days, ours to waste,
Over now, with too much haste.

Not lost on me now, the lessons learned,
Every day is a new page turned.
Above all else, I know for sure,
Those who I love, and love me, fill my thoughts.

I will not give another day
To wasted thoughts, just whiled away.
I'll fill each one with deeds well done,
As for regrets; there will be need for none.

4

School Holidays

Thank God, the last day of term is near,
We're winding down before a brand new year.
Some of my friends I won't see for weeks,
But others I'll message and send lots of tweets.

I hope we are going away somewhere,
Some sunshine and beaches and salty sea air.
I haven't heard any proper arrangements,
Mum wants the sun, Dad wants fields and tents.

Oh, please, please Mum, don't let Dad win,
The battle of the holiday choice; don't give in.
I couldn't stand the cold, damp night air,
And the lumpy ground would make me despair.

I want to feel the sun on my back,
Then walk along a hot sandy track.
We could even do a cultural tour,
I won't have a moan, I promise, for sure.

If we stay at home for the whole summer break,
I think I'll go mad, make no mistake.
We all need to get away for a rest,
I worked really hard at school in my tests.

My friend has just put up a message app note,
They're off to Spain in a villa, she wrote.
Can we do something similar to that?
We can sit by the pool and have mobile chats.

What do you mean, it makes no sense,
To go to all that huge expense?
To pay for a hotel with beautiful scenes,
And sit staring down at a mobile screen.

As I recall, each time I look,
You're sat by the pool, reading a book!
Maybe Dad has got it right,
Let's stay at home. You read and I'll write.

5

Popular

James is the most popular boy in our school,
Becky's the most popular girl and she's cool.
I wish I could be just like they are,
Respected, looked up to and treated like a star.

I'd have lots of new friends; they'd think I was great,
Whatever I said would carry some weight.
I'd rule the place; I'd be the boss,
That's how I'd get my views across.

I really think it's the very best way,
To make people like me and hear what I say.
To be the popular one in the school,
If you didn't want that, you'd just be a fool.

What could be better? I'd have loads of mates,
For me, a great school life that way awaits.
I wouldn't need the friends I've got now,
I'd find better ones and out they could bow.

My new best friends would be loyal and good,
They'd help and support me whenever they could,
At least I think they'd be like that,
Not liking me just because I'm the top cat.

Mind you, the friends I've got already
Are loyal, reliable and steady.
Perhaps my respect should be reserved,
For friends I've disrespected, which is undeserved.

When I think about my friends,
I really need to make amends,
If James and Becky only could
Be as lucky as me, with friends as good.

6

Best Friends

I sometimes wonder about my friends,
Are my choices based on latest trends?
Have I got enough of them, too many, too few?
I think my current best friend is you.

I think I have just the right amount,
But what would I do if we fell out?
Could I replace you with someone as good?
I doubt I'd want to, even if I could.

My friends online aren't here right now,
Could they support me? I don't see how.
I think to have you standing near,
Makes everything just seem clear.

Friends online are all very well,
But they're not here, when I have a secret to tell.
It just makes sense to keep you close,
It's you I want to talk to most.

Do I need you more than you need me?
I hope, for us, there's equity.
I hope you feel the same as I,
And never have to question why.

I realise why I like you now,
You don't need others to show you how.
You inspire me to be like you,
I'll take your lead, and like me too!

7

Falling Out

What happened there? What did I say?
For you to look the other way?
We're supposed to be the best of friends,
How could you just let that end?

Tell me what it was I said,
That made you glare and turn your head.
I didn't mean to cause you pain,
Just let me make it right again.

If I said something wrong, it wasn't meant,
I only spoke with good intent.
Please try to see from my point of view,
I would never want to offend you.

We've laughed, we've cried, we've shared it all,
We can't fall out over something so small.
Just talk to me; we can work this out,
Don't go online and scream and shout.

A private talk is all we need,
Please talk to me, don't make me read.
You've posted online for all to see,
Telling everybody you now hate me.

I couldn't be more hurt right now,
Let me put things right; just tell me how.
Can we please meet like we usually do?
We can talk it through, just we two.

Our friendship means too much to me.
To risk it all, so hear my plea.
I'll wait in the morning at our usual place,
And hope you turn up, to put your case.

Falling out is such a shame,
But it happens, and no-one's to blame.
There's nothing that can't be put right
Just sleep on it for now. Good night.

8

Friends Again

We're friends again, what a great feeling,
We needed some time, to help with the healing.
Our friendship had been all tattered and torn,
But we pulled ourselves back from the eye of the storm.

We've known each other since almost forever,
Our lasting friendship our greatest endeavour.
Your company feels like a warm, welcome breeze,
A safe, secure harbour from dangerous seas.

It doesn't matter what pulled us apart,
Just that we're able to make a fresh start.
I couldn't hate you, you couldn't hate me,
We're meant to be friends, and we always will be.

Next time it feels like there's something wrong,
Let's sit down and talk, not leave it so long.
We could have nipped this row in the bud,
But our silly pride left us stuck in the mud.

Never again will I let my hot head
Allow my loyalty to be misled.
Our friendship is far too precious for me
To put it at risk, I hope you'll agree.

9

My Mum

Is your mum like mine? Does she nag and fuss?
Does she tell you it's just that she cares so much?
'You can't go there, you can't go here,
Get that mobile away from your ear!'

One of these days, I'll be old enough
To get my own place; it can't be that tough.
I'll stay up late and watch TV,
With no-one there to watch over me.

I can have my friends over whenever I wish,
I'll eat chips out of paper, not washing a dish.
I'll play my music loud and thumping,
With nobody there to stop me jumping.

Life at my place will be so much fun,
Without the nagging of my mum,
It might not be the cleanest place,
Nor will it have much wardrobe space.

I'm sure I'll learn to cook my tea,
And buy new clothes when the whim takes me.
New shoes, mobiles, computer games,
Will simply appear, like now, just the same.

If it doesn't quite work out that way,
I can call up Mum, but what would I say?
'I'm sorry Mum, you weren't so bad,
I just didn't realise what I had.'

Perhaps I'll leave those plans a while,
Just for Mum, y'know, to make her smile.
How would she cope if I were gone?
No; I'll stay for her (but I won't let on).

10

My Family

"We're a very close family, they say on TV.
Good for you, what's it to me?
I can't stand it when they're all lovey-dovey,
They're probably rich and rolling in money.

My family's not like that, we argue and fight,
If one says it's black, the other says white.
I don't think it's likely we'll ever agree
It's just my family; we're like that, you see.

If we could be more like those ones on TV,
We'd go out to restaurants, or sit and have tea.
We'd eat together and talk of our day,
Then dig out a board game and laugh and play.

The truth is I'm not sure I'd like it like that,
I'm really quite happy when we're having a spat.
I can shout at my brother and moan at my mum,
I can sit back then; my work here is done!

They don't mind, I'm sure, as they get their own back,
When I do something wrong and they're on the attack.
I think it's quite healthy to disagree
On some small matters, it's plain to see.

We always remember, we're family, in the end,
We want to stay close; we want to be friends.
Would I really want things to be any different?
My love for my family nobody can dent.

All-in-all, I see it as luck,
To have the family with whom I'm stuck.
I think I should just sit and count my blessings,
Right where I've learnt my most valuable lessons.

11

I Have a Secret

I have a big secret which I cannot tell,
If people found out my life would be hell.
I can't even tell my dad or my mum,
If I tell anybody, I'll be struck dumb.

I'd love to tell my very best friend,
But if I do that, our friendship might end.
Should I tell a teacher at school?
I think if I do, they'll call me a fool.

I think about it first thing in the morning,
Then during the day, it appears without warning.
I'm worried sick, I have to say,
It follows me round the entire day.

When will I feel I've left it behind?
If it wasn't so bad, I don't think I'd mind.
I just want to be care-free again,
I'm not sure how long I can suffer the strain.

If I knew where to go, to off-load this stress,
I'd be there right now, to end my distress.
Can anybody help me; I'd love to know,
Just say where they are and I will go.

I have an idea, I'll write a letter,
I'll off-load this guilt and then I'll feel better.
I don't have to sign it; they won't know it's me,
For the first time in ages, I'll really be free.

Oh, what a feeling, I've put it in writing,
At my heels this secret is no longer biting.
I've done the right thing that much is clear,
The end of this nightmare is now very near

My teacher at school will read my letter,
A secret shared will make me feel better.
She'd help me, I know, without giving away,
The secret that's followed me every day.

12

In Confidence

My friend trusted me with a piece of big news,
I'd love to tell, but his friendship I'd lose.
I promised him I'd keep his secret,
Until he's ready to reveal it.

It's killing me though; I don't mind saying,
I'd love to shout out, on my mind it's playing,
A good friend, however, would not give away,
A confidence shared, at the end of the day.

He's kept lots of secrets of mine all these years,
Good things and bad things, hopes and fears.
He's trusted me with this secret today,
It would be wrong to give it away.

It's not a bad thing though, I have to point out,
In fact, if you knew it, you'd share it about.
I don't know why he's keeping it quiet,
If it was me, I'd be having a riot!

It's his choice though, I've promised to hush,
If everyone knew, it would make him blush.
I can't wait, however, to share the good news,
But until then, to talk I'll refuse.

Oh, hurry up! I'm dying to share
Your fabulous news; right now I don't dare.
What's that? They now know? You've already told?
I wanted to share it, my news is now cold.

I suppose it was always your news to give,
It was never for me, so you I forgive.
A confidence that I was happy to keep,
Confirming our friendship is solid and deep.

Lesson Plans

There are lesson plans structured around the subject matter in each poem.

For the purposes of these plans, it is assumed that the lesson will last for one hour, although there is no obligation to use the timescale of the plan.

In writing these plans, I have sought to identify the lessons and values which I believe can to be learned from each poem. As a professional teacher, however, you may discover other areas, or merits, in the poems that you feel you can draw on, or which can accommodate a group discussion.

You may choose to use your existing lesson plan format, or to adjust the one provided, so that it is more aligned to your existing plan.

Most of the lessons will end with the students being asked to write their own short poem, but this may be set as a homework task, even where the lesson plans do not ask for a poem to be written during class.

Copies of the lesson plans can be downloaded for printing by visiting the website: www.jayclarkebooks.com

Poem 1 – The Bully and the Bullied

Subject:			Resource:		
PSHE (Personal, Social, Health and Economic Education)			BOOK (Poetry for PSHE by Jay Clarke)		
Teacher:		**Date:**		**Group size:**	

Direction

Topic: Bullying and remedies
This is a dual poem, "The Bully and the Bullied", intended to be read by two people. In this scenario-based activity, the class should be divided into two groups, with one student from each group being called to read out aloud. One side should take the part of the bully and, the other, the bullied
The dual poem will be introduced and a "virtual" fight of words will take place. At the end of the session, the class will vote on who took the moral high ground and who won or lost the battle of words.
Lesson Aims:
To introduce the idea that disputes can be resolved by words, rather than violence or threats. To encourage debate about the effects of bullying and the futility of it. To try to understand the reason why the bully in the poem did what he did.

Generic learning outcomes:	Differentiated learning outcomes:
By the end of the session, learners will be able to-	*Learners with more advanced current skills will be able to-*
Identify the reasons behind some forms of bullying. Apportion responsibility. Suggest resolution methods.	Analyse the underlying problems that some bullies are trying to mask. Give help and advice to those being bullied.

Key Skills Development

Communication / Literacy / Reading	Wider Key Skills
All class will be required to read at least one half of the poem.	Dispute resolution. Decision-making, discussing options.

Time	Teacher activity	Student activity	
2.30-2.45	Hand out the dual poem and divide the class into two groups: one representing the bully, the other the bullied. Ask one student from each side to volunteer to role-play/ read out their half of the poem and the responses.	After reviewing the poem(s) on an overhead projector or whiteboard, each volunteer student will read out his section of poetry, interleaving it with his or her opposing player/reader.	Book of poetry, projector and/or
2.45 – 3.05	Ask questions of the students, including which "side" they agree with, and why. Ask the students who appears to "win" the battle of words, based solely on the poem.	Students engage in a group discussion about the exchanges between the two students in the poem and whether they could have used different expressions to get their points across.	Students
3.05 – 3.15	Ask students to write short (four line) poem, imagining themselves as a mediator, giving advice to the bully and their victim.	Students are asked to write at least four lines of poetry, to be completed within 10 minutes.	Pen and paper or writing book.
3.15 – 3.30	Introduce group discussion.	Discuss what they have learned about bullying and how they would handle a bullying situation.	Students
Session Evaluation: *Consider what went well, areas for improvement, points to take forward*			

Poem 2 – Safe House

Subject: Education		Resource:	
PSHE (Personal, Social, Health and Economic Education)		BOOK (Poetry for PSHE by Jay Clarke)	
Teacher:	**Date:**	**Group size:**	

Direction

Topic: Bullying and remedies
The poem "Safe House" is written from the point of view of somebody being pursued by bullies, desperate to get home to their "safe house". It builds up to a sense of fear before questioning what can be done.

Lesson Aims:
To encourage students to explore how it feels to be bullied and how to deal with it, including who to discuss it with.

Generic learning outcomes:	Differentiated learning outcomes:
By the end of the session, learners will be able to-	*Learners with more advanced current skills will be able to-*
Determine whether they identify with the writer, or have been bullied themselves, and how they handled the situation.	Give suggestions about how this situation can be handled and who a person being bullied can talk to. They may also be able to advise a bully about the consequences of their actions.

Key Skills Development

Communication / Literacy / Reading	Wider Key Skills
The class are required to read the entire poem; reading out loud if preferred.	Empathy, dispute resolution, discussion and debate.

Time	Teacher activity	Student activity	Resources
2.30-2.45	Show poem on overhead projector or whiteboard, with a short introduction. Ask students for their initial thoughts.	Review the poem and volunteer views about its content.	Book of poetry, projector and/or whiteboard. Use handouts, if necessary.
2.45 – 3.05	Ask one (or several) student(s) to read the poem out loud. Question: Can you empathise with the writer?	A student (or several in turn) reads the poem out loud.	Students
3.05 – 3.15	Question: Can you empathise with the writer? Question: What is meant here by "safe house"? Question: Whose house is it?	The student(s) should try to put themselves in the place of the writer and say whether or not they empathise and whether they have fully understood the poem.	Students
3.15 – 3.30	Question: Who could the writer have spoken to? Question: What would you do in this situation?	Students should offer advice on where a person can turn when they are being bullied and how they would handle the situation.	Students

Session Evaluation: *Consider what went well, areas for improvement, points to take forward*

Poem 3 – School Days

Subject:		Resource:	
PSHE (Personal, Social, Health and Economic Education)		BOOK (Poetry for PSHE by Jay Clarke)	
Teacher:	Date:	Group size:	

Direction

Topic: School and retrospection
The poem "School Days" is written by an adult, looking back nostalgically to their school days.
Lesson Aims:
To encourage the students to look some years ahead and imagine themselves as the writer. They can compare the favourable view of the writer's school days with the view they have at present.

Generic learning outcomes:	Differentiated learning outcomes:
By the end of the session, learners will be able to-	*Learners with more advanced current skills will be able to-*
Determine whether or not the writer's view holds with theirs, as well as discuss whether or not they believe school days have changed over time.	Discuss why the writer's memories are (or appear to be) more or less favourable than those of themselves and their peers. Defend a position of being an adult and recognising the value, not only of school itself, but the enjoyment of those days.

Key Skills Development

Communication / Literacy / Reading	Wider Key Skills
The class are required to read the entire poem; reading out loud if preferred. Retrospection. Nostalgia.	Historical debate and progressive exchange of views. Retrospection. Nostalgia.

Time	Teacher activity	Student activity	Resources
2.30-2.45	Show poem on overhead projector or whiteboard, with a short introduction. Ask students for their initial thoughts.	Review the poem and volunteer views about its content.	Book of poetry, projector and/ or whiteboard. Use handouts, if necessary.
2.45 – 3.05	Question: How many students walk to school, as opposed to being given lifts? Question: At what age might students walk to school alone?	Talk about what age they were when they first walked to school on their own. Did they prefer it? Did they call for a friend on the way? Did they feel safe?	Students
3.05 – 3.15	Ask students whether, given the opportunity, they would write favourably or not about their own school days. Ask them to write a short poem.	Students should engage in a discussion around the question and then write a short poem of their own, entitled "My School Days"	Pen and paper or writing book.
3.15 – 3.30	Question: Does the writer appear to enjoy the time, or do students think the writer only appears to enjoy that time in retrospect?	Students should engage in a discussion around the question and are invited to read out their poems to the rest of the class.	Students
Session Evaluation: *Consider what went well, areas for improvement, points to take forward*			

Poem 4 – School Holidays

Subject:		Resource:	
PSHE (Personal, Social, Health and Economic Education)		BOOK (Poetry for PSHE by Jay Clarke)	
Teacher:	Date:	Group size:	

Direction

Topic: School times and holiday times
The poem "School Holidays" reflects how a student imagines they'd like to spend their upcoming school holidays. It also explores their relationship with their parents.
Lesson Aims:
To encourage students to consider the wants and needs of different family members and consider whether they could adjust their normal behaviour to make other family members happy.

Generic learning outcomes:	Differentiated learning outcomes:
By the end of the session, learners will be able to-	*Learners with more advanced current skills will be able to-*
Identify the different needs of family members and agree on whether or not there was a successful outcome.	Discuss the reasonableness, or otherwise of the writer, and their consideration for their parents.

Key Skills Development

Communication / Literacy / Reading	Wider Key Skills
The class are required to read the entire poem; reading out loud if preferred.	Compromising. Dispute resolution.

Time	Teacher activity	Student activity	Resources
2.30-2.45	Show poem on overhead projector or whiteboard, with a short introduction. Ask students for their initial thoughts.	Review the poem and volunteer views about its content.	Book of poetry, projector and/ or whiteboard. Use handouts, if necessary.
2.45 – 3.05	Question: Is the writer looking forward to their holiday? Question: Of the two types, what would be your choice?	Engage in group discussion, answering questions.	Students
3.05 – 3.15	Question: Do you think the holiday went ahead? Question: Why might it not happen?	Discuss the concerns of the parents. Discuss the fairness of the mobile phone issue.	Students
3.15 – 3.30	Ask student to put themselves in the position of the father and write a short poem in support.	Write a short poem, putting the father's view across and "selling" the idea of a camping holiday.	Pen and paper or writing book.

Session Evaluation: *Consider what went well, areas for improvement, points to take forward*

Poem 5 – Popular

Subject:		Resource:	
PSHE (Personal, Social, Health and Economic Education)		BOOK (Poetry for PSHE by Jay Clarke)	
Teacher:	**Date:**	**Group size:**	

Direction

Topic: Schools, social engagement and popularity
The poem "Popular" describes a student extolling the virtues of the two most popular people in their school and appearing to envy them.
Lesson Aims:
To consider and discuss the merits of popularity and the writer's initial wish to be like others who are more popular. To form an opinion about the value, or otherwise, of being popular.

Generic learning outcomes:	Differentiated learning outcomes:
By the end of the session, learners will be able to-	*Learners with more advanced current skills will be able to-*
Separate the perceived popularity of some students and the actual value of others' status and friendships.	Establish whether it is reasonable to hold some peers in higher esteem than others and the effect this has on some.

Key Skills Development

Communication / Literacy / Reading	Wider Key Skills
The class are required to read the entire poem; reading out loud if preferred.	Respect. Social development.

Time	Teacher activity	Student activity	Resources
2.30-2.45	Show poem on overhead projector or whiteboard, with a short introduction. Ask students for their initial thoughts.	Review the poem and volunteer views about its content.	Book of poetry, projector and/or whiteboard. Use handouts, if necessary.
2.45 – 3.05	Question: Why does the writer appear to respect James and Becky so much?	Engage in group discussion about what makes some people more popular than others.	Students
3.05 – 3.15	Question: Is the writer being fair on their existing friends? If not, why not?	Discuss the value of friendship and say how they would feel if they were the writer's friend and they read this.	Students
3.15 – 3.30	Ask students to write a poem, imagining they are James or Becky, wishing they were somebody else!	Students should write a short poem.	Pen and paper or writing book.

Session Evaluation: *Consider what went well, areas for improvement, points to take forward*

Poem 6 – Best Friends

Subject:		Resource:	
PSHE (Personal, Social, Health and Economic)		BOOK (Poetry for PSHE by Jay Clarke)	
Teacher:	**Date:**	**Group size:**	

Direction

Topic: Friendship
The poem "Best Friends" is about the writer's friends. The writer also considers their choice of "best friend".
Lesson Aims:
To encourage students to consider what they want (or perceive they need) from friendship. To discuss the contrasting values that different people can bring to a social group.

Generic learning outcomes:	Differentiated learning outcomes:
By the end of the session, learners will be able to-	*Learners with more advanced current skills will be able to-*
Understand the value of a good friendship. Identify the nuances within the poem, where the writer finally understands the value of their existing friends.	Discuss the purpose and complexity of changing friends and motives for doing so.

Key Skills Development

Communication / Literacy / Reading	Wider Key Skills
The class are required to read the entire poem; reading out loud if preferred.	Social awareness, respect, empathy and consideration of others' feelings.

Time	Teacher activity	Student activity	Resources
2.30-2.45	Show poem on overhead projector or whiteboard, with a short introduction. Ask students for their initial thoughts.	Review the poem and volunteer views about its content.	Book of poetry, projector and/ or whiteboard. Use handouts, if necessary.
2.45 – 3.05	Question: Does it matter how many friends the writer has? Question: Does the writer appreciate their existing friends by the end of the poem?	Engage in group discussion about whether the number of friends should matter more than the quality.	Students
3.05 – 3.15	Question: Have you ever considered "dropping" one or more friends and why? Question: Is it normal to change friends as time goes by and if so, under what circumstances?	Answer questions about why they would let go of a friend. Explain why friends may change over a long period of time and why some people keep friends for a long time, or for life.	Pen/Paper
3.15 – 3.30	Ask students to write a short poem about their own friends and explain why they have a best friend, if they do.	Write a poem and read it out aloud, if time permits.	Pen and paper or writing book.

Session Evaluation: *Consider what went well, areas for improvement, points to take forward*

Poem 7 – Falling Out

Subject:		Resource:	
PSHE (Personal, Social, Health and Economic Education)		BOOK (Poetry for PSHE by Jay Clarke)	
Teacher:	**Date:**	**Group size:**	

Direction

Topic: Friendship and dispute resolution	
The poem "Falling Out" is about falling out with a friend. It examines the writer's confusion about the reason for the fall-out and their desire to make amends.	
Lesson Aims:	
To discuss how disputes develop and why people sometimes fall out as a result. Discuss the futility of allowing a small matter to spoil a friendship and the pain it may cause. Offer dispute resolution techniques.	
Generic learning outcomes: *By the end of the session, learners will be able to-*	**Differentiated learning outcomes:** *Learners with more advanced current skills will be able to-*
Identify how easy it may be to fall out with somebody and how to be aware of the signs of a dispute early on.	Manage a conflict between others and bring a dispute to resolution.

Key Skills Development

Communication / Literacy / Reading	Wider Key Skills
The class are required to read the entire poem; reading out loud if preferred.	Conflict management, dispute resolution and intervention.

Time	Teacher activity	Student activity	Resources
2.30-2.45	Show poem on overhead projector or whiteboard, with a short introduction. Ask students for their initial thoughts.	Review the poem and volunteer views about its content.	Book of poetry, projector and/or whiteboard. Use handouts, if necessary.
2.45 – 3.05	Question: What do you think could have happened to make these two friends fall out? Question: How hard is the writer trying to resolve the matter?	Students should identify parts in the poem where they believe they see a possible reason for the fall-out. They should also identify the areas where the writer tries to make amends.	Students
3.05 – 3.15	Question: Have you ever fallen out with a friend or family member, and why? Question: Were you able to make up again, and how?	Students volunteer anecdotes about falling out with somebody close to them. They also offer solutions they found to make up, or explain why it wasn't possible.	Students
3.15 – 3.30	Invite students to write a short poem, imagining themselves as the writer's friend; the one who has been hurt and explaining to the writer why they were angry and what they expect now.	Students should write a short poem about their feelings towards a friend who they feel has let them down, and tell that friend what they now expect, in order to make amends.	Pen and paper or writing book.

Session Evaluation: *Consider what went well, areas for improvement, points to take forward*

Poem 8 – Friends Again

Subject:		Resource:	
PSHE (Personal, Social, Health and Economic Education)		BOOK (Poetry for PSHE by Jay Clarke)	
Teacher:	**Date:**	**Group size:**	

Direction

Topic: Friendship and dispute resolution
The poem "Friends Again" is an upbeat response to the earlier poem "Falling Out", about a dispute with a best friend. It explores the feelings of relief and touches on some of the techniques used to bring about a resolution.
Lesson Aims:
To demonstrate how a conflict, regardless of how serious it first appears, can be resolved and how the resolution was brought about. It also identifies the writer's plans to avoid such disputes in the future.

Generic learning outcomes:	Differentiated learning outcomes:
By the end of the session, learners will be able to-	*Learners with more advanced current skills will be able to-*
Identify with a desire to resolve a dispute and find areas of common ground which can be used to help bring about a resolution.	Discuss with others what they have in common, rather than what divides them and to be able to engage in dispute resolution.

Key Skills Development

Communication / Literacy / Reading	Wider Key Skills
The class are required to read the entire poem; reading out loud if preferred.	Conflict management. Dispute resolution.

Time	Teacher activity	Student activity	Resources
2.30-2.45	Show poem on overhead projector or whiteboard, with a short introduction. Ask students for their initial thoughts.	Review the poem and volunteer views about its content.	Book of poetry, projector and/or whiteboard. Use handouts, if necessary.
2.45 – 3.05	Question: In the third verse, the writer says, "It doesn't matter what pulled us apart". Do you agree? Are some reasons worse than others? Is there anything that can't be forgiven?	Students engage in a group discussion about the severity of some comments that a friend might make that would upset them, or whether they really believe some things cannot be forgiven.	Students
3.05 – 3.15	Invite students to share a story about falling out with somebody (if not a friend, a family member), which was resolved. Ask who made the first move, and how.	Students give examples of when they have managed to resolve an argument with somebody and who they feel should make the first move.	Pen/Paper
3.15 – 3.30	Question: What if these two friends hadn't made up? What could be the consequences of a long-standing dispute between the two friends, as well as those around them?	Students engage in a group discussion about long-standing disputes and how they might escalate, even as far as never being able to make up. Explain how others are also effected.	Pen and paper or writing book.

Session Evaluation: *Consider what went well, areas for improvement, points to take forward*

Poem 9 – My Mum

Subject:	Resource:
PSHE (Personal, Social, Health and Economic)	BOOK (Poetry for PSHE by Jay Clarke)

Teacher:	Date:	Group size:

Direction

Topic: Families
The poem "My Mum" is about the writer's relationship with their mother and how they imagine life will be without her in their home. The writer explores what is possible for them now and how they perceive it might be otherwise.

Lesson Aims:
To encourage students to explore their own relationships and to identify the irony of their assertions as the poem unfolds.

Generic learning outcomes:	Differentiated learning outcomes:
By the end of the session, learners will be able to-	*Learners with more advanced current skills will be able to-*
Identify which parts of the poem are reasonable and fair and identify the parts they disagree with, offering alternative thoughts.	Offer alternative views in support of the mother. Explain whether or not the writer would really be better off in the world they describe and why.

Key Skills Development

Communication / Literacy / Reading	Wider Key Skills
The class are required to read the entire poem; reading out loud if preferred.	Consideration, social awareness, respect. Irony.

Time	Teacher activity	Student activity	Resources
2.30-2.45	Show poem on overhead projector or whiteboard, with a short introduction. Ask students for their initial thoughts.	Review the poem and volunteer views about its content.	Book of poetry, projector and/or whiteboard. Use handouts, if necessary.
2.45 – 3.05	Question: Can you identify with the writer, in the case of the adult(s) in your life? Question: Do you sometimes feel like this towards the adult(s) in your life?	Students engage in a group discussion about the parts of the poem they feel they can and can't identify with, giving reasons why.	Students
3.05 – 3.15	Questions: At what stage do you think the writer starts to become aware that their current lifestyle might not be so bad?	Students engage in a group discussion about how they read the poem and where they found the writer had turned a little, to recognise the positive aspects of their relationship.	Pen/Paper
3.15 – 3.30	Invite students to write a short poem about the adult(s) in their lives, concentrating on only the positive things they bring to their relationship.	Students write a short poem, highlighting the good things about the relationship they have with the adult(s) in their lives.	Pen and paper or writing book.

Session Evaluation: *Consider what went well, areas for improvement, points to take forward*

Poem 10 – My Family

Subject:		Resource:	
PSHE (Personal, Social, Health and Economic Education)		BOOK (Poetry for PSHE by Jay Clarke)	
Teacher:	**Date:**	**Group size:**	

Direction

Topic: Families
The poem "My Family" is about the writer's family and how they compare with other families, on TV or elsewhere.
Lesson Aims:
To encourage students to explore their view of their own family, selecting the parts of the poem they can identify with.

Generic learning outcomes:	Differentiated learning outcomes:
By the end of the session, learners will be able to-	*Learners with more advanced current skills will be able to-*
Offer opinions on positives and negatives in the poem. Explain whether or not the writer's perception of their family is a favourable one.	Explain, from the writer's point of view, how they appear to recognise positive aspects of family life as the poem progresses.

Key Skills Development

Communication / Literacy / Reading	Wider Key Skills
The class are required to read the entire poem; reading out loud if preferred.	Empathy, debating, positive framing.

Time	Teacher activity	Student activity	Resources
2.30-2.45	Show poem on overhead projector or whiteboard, with a short introduction. Ask students for their initial thoughts.	Review the poem and volunteer views about its content.	Book of poetry, projector and/or whiteboard. Use handouts, if necessary.
2.45 – 3.05	Question: Is your family like the ones the writer sees on TV ("very close" and "all lovey-dovey"), or like the writer's own ("we argue and fight")?	Students respond with their opinion of which type of family they believe they have.	Students
3.05 – 3.15	Question: Do you think any family can be like the TV families all the time? Question: Do you think the writer's family is probably just like the TV families really?	Students engage in a group discussion about the perception of what family life is like and how it might differ from the reality.	Pen/Paper
3.15 – 3.30	Invite students to choose one side or the other (happy families, or those who "argue and fight") and write a short poem, describing their family.	Students write a short poem, describing their fictional family and highlighting the good or bad points.	Pen and paper or writing book.

Session Evaluation: *Consider what went well, areas for improvement, points to take forward*

Poem 11 – I Have a Secret

Subject:		Resource:
PSHE (Personal, Social, Health and Economic)		BOOK (Poetry for PSHE by Jay Clarke)
Teacher:	**Date:**	**Group size:**

Direction

Topic: Secrets and confidences
The poem "I Have a Secret" tells of the writer's angst about the responsibility of a secret they are keeping, without ever explaining what the secret is.
Lesson Aims:
To encourage students to imagine being inside the head of the writer, trying to understand their feelings of anxiety and offering suggestions about what the secret may be. They may also discuss how the writer might off-load some of their anxiety.

Generic learning outcomes:	Differentiated learning outcomes:
By the end of the session, learners will be able to-	*Learners with more advanced current skills will be able to-*
Empathise with the writer. Understand what may be the severity of the secret. Offer suggestions about how to handle the stress of the situation.	Determine whether or not the writer should, in fact, be so anxious and recognise how conflated a subject can seem, depending on a person's association with it.

Key Skills Development

Communication / Literacy / Reading	Wider Key Skills
The class are required to read the entire poem; reading out loud if preferred.	Listening, empathising, and advising. Hyperbole.

Time	Teacher activity	Student activity	Resources
2.30-2.45	Show poem on overhead projector or whiteboard, with a short introduction. Ask students for their initial thoughts.	Review the poem and volunteer views about its content.	Book of poetry, projector and/or whiteboard. Use handouts, if necessary.
2.45 – 3.05	Question: What do you think his secret could be? Question: Why might this secret end the writer's friendship?	Students engage in a group discussion about what they believe this secret could be and develop that to imagine why it would affect the writer's friendship.	Students
3.05 – 3.15	Question: Does the writer have any idea of how they can off-load this secret? If so, how? Question: The writer thinks they can share it with their teacher, but then changes their mind. Why?	Students should identify areas of the poem where they think the writer has mentioned, or hinted, how they think they can end their distress, and who they might talk to.	Pen/Paper
3.15 – 3.30	Invite students to write a short poem, imagining themselves to be the teacher, and encouraging the writer to speak to them.	Write a short poem, as the teacher, urging the writer to unburden themselves of the stress of keeping the secret. Assure the writer that it is in their interest to do so.	Pen and paper or writing book.
Session Evaluation: *Consider what went well, areas for improvement, points to take forward*			

Poem 12 – In Confidence

Subject:		Resource:	
PSHE (Personal, Social, Health and Economic Education)		BOOK (Poetry for PSHE by Jay Clarke)	
Teacher:	**Date:**	**Group size:**	

Direction

Topic: Secrets and confidences
The poem "In Confidence" is written from the perspective of somebody who has been trusted to keep a confidence by a friend. It explores the loyalty of the friend in keeping the confidence, whilst showing their desire to share it.
Lesson Aims:

Generic learning outcomes:	Differentiated learning outcomes:
By the end of the session, learners will be able to-	*Learners with more advanced current skills will be able to-*
Determine whether or not the writer has honoured their friend by managing to keep their confidence, thereby showing a degree of loyalty and maturity.	Identify with the writer's urge to share the information, while wanting to stay loyal. Debate the writer's frustration at the news having already been shared before they got to share it.

Key Skills Development

Communication / Literacy / Reading	Wider Key Skills
The class are required to read the entire poem; reading out loud if preferred.	Confidentiality, irony.

Time	Teacher activity	Student activity	Resources
2.30-2.45	Show poem on overhead projector or whiteboard, with a short introduction. Ask students for their initial thoughts.	Review the poem and volunteer views about its content.	Book of poetry, projector and/or whiteboard. Use handouts, if necessary.
2.45 – 3.05	Question: Have you ever been given a piece of news you're dying to tell, but you're asked not to? Question: Did you manage to keep the confidence? If not, why not?	Students offer anecdotal incidences of holding onto news they'd like to announce. They may also offer incidences where confidences were broken, and say why.	Students
3.05 – 3.15	Question: What are some of the reasons the writer gives for wanting to tell? Question: Why do you think the writer didn't tell? Question: Was the writer frustrated in the end?	Students refer to the statements given in the poem for why the writer felt an urge to announce the news, why they didn't and how they felt in the end.	Pen/Paper
3.15 – 3.30	Question: Why is it important to keep a confidence? Question: Under what circumstances would you feel you couldn't keep a confidence?	Students engage in a group discussion about the importance of confidentiality. They may also discuss when it might not be sensible or safe to keep something confidential.	Pen and paper or writing book.

Session Evaluation: *Consider what went well, areas for improvement, points to take forward*